Night Shift

Night Shift

MAINTAINING HEALTH AND WELLNESS

Audrey F. Thomas

This book is dedicated to all night-shift workers and their families.

This book is written with night-shift workers in mind, but anyone struggling with lack of sleep or chronic sleep loss can benefit from reading this book.

Contents

Acknowledgments

Thanks to my Lord and Savior, Jesus Christ, for the desire long ago to write a book.

Thanks to my husband, Gerald, for giving me the time to write this book. Thanks to Melissa S. my accountability partner, for holding me accountable to reach incremental goals in writing, editing, and publishing, and for listening and providing suggestions and critiquing the manuscript..

Thank you, Armand, for your part of editing your Aunt Audrey's manuscript.

Thanks to Vanessa for being a sounding board and for her constructive suggestions and critiques.

Thanks to Best Buy Geek Squad for help with computer & document issues

Thanks to friends and family for prayer, support, and encouragement.

Thanks to the IIN community for support and encouragement.

Last, but not least, to Joshua and Lindsey for the "Launch Your Dream Book" course.

Introduction

Night-shift or rotational-shift work is common and germane to today's society. Corporations and organizations utilize a twenty-four-hour scheduling format to service their needs, especially the needs of companies that provide service to the public. Unfortunately, night-shift or rotational-shift workers are faced with risks as they work these nights or rotational shifts. I have worked the night shift for more than twenty-five years as a registered nurse and now as a health coach. I have encountered some of these risks and have developed strategies for addressing them.

Night-shift workers receive a shift differential incentive that provides some financial advantage over day-shift work. Unfortunately, shift workers face changes in their circadian cycles that result in sleep loss, sleep deprivation, and over time, health risks. Becoming knowledgeable about night-shift work and its effects on the body and implementing strategies to address sleep loss and ensure adequate sleep assist the night-shift worker to avoid sleep deprivation. This book also addresses the sleep and nutritional needs of the night-shift worker, along with why it is necessary for family, friends, and corporations to understand the needs of the night-shift worker. In this book I outline some of my struggles as a shift worker, sharing some of my strategies that I have spent many years developing. It is my hope that the reader will reflect on his or her experiences and work on strategies to help maintain health and wellness.

Everyone needs to weigh the risks versus his or her needs for working the night shift. For some, rotating to the night shift is mandatory, and knowing how to maintain health and address sleep needs is essential. Others may have the option to change from night shift to day shift. This book is written for night-shift workers and anyone who is not getting enough good quality sleep.

History of Night-Shift Work

The night shift or shift work has been a practice for workers to cover blocks of hours of work post daylight for hundreds of years. Some past night-shift occupations have included ranchers guarding cattle. Present-day jobs such as industrial workers, truckers, manufacturers, air traffic controllers, offshore workers, health-care workers, and workers at service organizations require night-shift workers to cover the schedule in the evening and night hours for the continual needs or operation of companies. Michael Price (2011) reported that millions of Americans work permanent night shifts or rotate in and out of the night shift.

Typical night-shift schedules are from 11:00 p.m. to 7:00 a.m. (an eight-hour shift) or from 7:00 p.m. to 7:00 a.m., a twelve-hour shift. Night-shift hours worked usually consist of eight- or twelve-hour blocks of hours. The needs or management practices of the organization or company determine the hours selected for the night shift. Some hospital emergency rooms employ a 2:00 p.m. to 2:00 a.m. shift.

Whichever variation of shifts is used by companies, millions of people, for various reasons, work the night shift. Some companies feel it necessary to have employees rotate day and night shifts. Regardless, the night shift is a permanent part of businesses' staffing needs. Millions of medical personnel, police officers, firefighters, truckers, packing company employees, and others work these shifts. Workers choose these hours for many reasons such as worker suitability for the night shift, the need or desire for the shift differential or additional compensation to work the night shift, or to fill in holes in the schedule when call-ins result or the workload increases. Whatever the reason, millions of employees around the globe work the night shift.

The Night Shift: My Beginning

was a very light sleeper as a teenager. Any little noise woke me up. Once awake it was hard to fall asleep again.

After having children I did not get much sleep at night. Nighttime feedings, especially breast-feeding, promoted very little sleep time. As a result I experienced sleepiness and fatigue as I worked the day shift. I had gotten used to being awake at night. My sleep-wake times had been reversed.

So I decided, since I had to be awake at night, I might as well get paid for it. I slept well during the day after I worked at night and was able to sleep well at night on my off days for more than twenty years. Then slowly I began to have a lot of sleepiness when I worked at night and had difficulty getting more than three hours of continuous sleep time during the day. When I wanted to sleep, I rested but my mind kept going; I kept thinking about the children, grandchildren, issues, and so on. Two times I had to come off the night shift for a year each time to regain the ability to sleep six or eight hours continuously, after which I was able to transition back to night-shift work. I remember years ago I had trouble sleeping and researched natural foods and drinks to help sleep and boost serotonin levels. The strategies worked, but when I no longer had trouble sleeping, I forgot about the natural products.

Some people are more suited to night-shift work compared to others. Those who have trouble staying awake at night and those who become physically ill should not work night shifts. A routine of regular sleep/wakefulness helps to provide some normalcy or structure for life and family times.

When I was a student in the health-coach program at the Institute for Integrative Nutrition®, we were often encouraged to reflect about the experiences that had a major impact on our lives and what measures we used to achieve health and wellness. As a night-shift worker, I did not realize my intermittent bouts of communication issues and becoming easily frustrated and angry were a result of lack of sleep. I was only sleeping three hours day or night. Finally, being called into the manager's office caused me to sit back, reflect, and pray for wisdom to find out what was going on. I knew I was having occasional issues, but I did not realize how much. I developed plans to do whatever was necessary to obtain eight hours of sleep. It is amazing how much more focus and memory improvement results from adequate sleep.

Circadian Rhythm

Every day our body cycles through periods of sleep and wakefulness. This cycling is not by chance or accident; our body is governed by a circadian clock or rhythm. Our circadian rhythm, according to Price (2011), "lets various glands know when to release hormones and control mood, alertness, body temperature, and other aspects of the body's daily cycle." Of particular importance to the night-shift worker is the hormone called melatonin. Melatonin is provided primarily from the pineal gland and also by dietary means.

"The pineal gland's only hormone, melatonin, is produced and released based its registering to light. Melatonin maintains the circadian rhythm and regulates reproductive hormones" (Sargis, 2014) such as estrogen. Our twenty-four-hour cycle of sleep/wake pattern is dic tated or influenced by daylight and darkness. "Light exposure stops the release of melatonin and helps to control our circadian rhythm" (Ibid.).

The night shift worker's sleep/wake cycle runs opposite to the natural circadian cycle, thereby presenting risks that day-shift workers do not encounter. When I began working the night shift, I did not know that excessive sleepiness, restlessness, insomnia, and fatigue were common issues faced by workers on the night shift, even though those were the very symptoms I was experiencing. Nor did I know that after years of working the night shift, the worker could be faced with disruption of the digestive and/or metabolic process, weight gain, decreased cognitive function and memory, and diminished ability to fight off infections. Individuals who rotate the day and night shift have more difficulty adjusting to alterations in their sleep/wake cycles compared to individuals who work the night shift permanently.

Night shifters sleep during the day. This flip-flop of rest and alert time runs counter to our natural circadian rhythm of sleeping when it is dark and being awake during the day. Knowing the risks of night-shift work allows the night-shift worker to develop and adopt measures to address the risks of working the night shift. It may take employees some time to adjust to the night shift. Sleepiness on the job is often addressed by drinking coffee or other caffeinated beverages. I used to cherish my cup of java until, at age twenty-nine; I developed a heart arrhythmia called premature atrial contractions as a result of caffeine sensitivity. Caffeinated drinks were no longer an option. I looked into herbal non-caffeine drinks. Some people develop jitteriness or trouble sleeping if too much coffee or caffeinated drink is consumed too close to sleep time. Other people have told me that coffee does not have an effect on them at all.

It is not uncommon to hear that after rough or extremely busy night shifts, driving while sleepy or falling asleep at the wheel has resulted in accidents, some of which have been fatal. That is why I have, periodically, called my husband to pick me up at work when I did not think I could make it home safely, or I took some time to rest in the car before driving home.

Night shifters must determine their sleep needs and actively pursue measures to accommodate them. Otherwise fatigue, restlessness, and insomnia can become problems. Insomnia often occurs after numerous shifts are worked in a row or from not allowing oneself to get enough sleep in-between or after night shifts worked. Sleep deprivation adds up until one cannot settle down to sleep to rest the mind or the body.

The Night Shift and It's
Effect on the Body

After decades of working the night shift, subtle changes in metabolism start to occur. If we are not proactive in a healthy lifestyle and in meeting sleep needs, then changes in digestion and metabolic function and weight gain start to occur. Weight gain, coupled with sleep deprivation or lack of sleep in a dark environment, opens the door for other health issues to occur. People who are faced with chronic sleep deprivation experience subtle changes in memory and cognitive function; they may wonder if it is simply a normal part of aging. Unhealthy lifestyles and inadequate sleep lead the way for succumbing to illnesses.

According to Kaczor(2010) melatonin release blocks estrogen and is switched off with light exposure. Working at night necessitates having the lights on. While working at night the body is not releasing melatonin and therefore estrogen isn't blocked. Unchecked estrogen release eventually promotes the growth of cancer, especially cancer of the breast (lbid). The World Health Organization has indicated that nocturnal work "is probably carcinogenic to humans" (lbid). Consider your sleep environment as a measure needed to keep estrogen levels in check because sleeping in a dark environment is paramount to melatonin release. Also, see appendix 3 & 4 for preparing the body to be inhospitable to cancer.

Weight gain is common in night-shift workers due to changes in carbohydrate metabolism, excess caloric intake, heavy meals, high simple carbohydrate intake, lack of exercise, and lack of sleep. Maintaining weight in recommended ranges remains a primary method of avoiding the associated health risks of obesity. The night-shift worker who is overweight or obese compounds the risks of working the night shift. According to the American Heart Association (2015), women should maintain their waist circumference less than thirty-five inches and men should keep their waist circumference less than forty inches for optimal health. See Appendix 1 for information on weight loss and Appendix 2 for strategies for effective weight loss.

Shift work is a fact of life. Someone has to work the night shift. Knowledge is power. A proactive approach can lessen, minimize, or ameliorate the risks of night-shift work and promote as much health and wellness as possible.

The next chapters address the purpose of sleep, sleep needs, healthy measures to maintain wakefulness during the night shift, and development of action plans that can be adopted to promote health and wellness.

The Purpose of Sleep

The purpose of sleep is many-faceted. According to "Importance of Sleep: Six Reasons Not to Scrimp on Sleep" (2006), sleep or the lack thereof affects memory and learning, weight and metabolism, mood, safety, and cardiovascular health. Sleep enhances commitment of new information to memory, problem-solving skills, and critical thinking. Work situations are handled professionally. Challenging shifts or customers are managed with satisfactory results. Cognitive function is at its peak. Sleep is the time in which the body repairs itself and recovery from illness or disease is enhanced.

Fatigue and sleep deprivation make it harder to remember new information. Adequate sleep assists the body to process and store carbohydrates and facilitates normal levels of appetite-supporting hormones. Chronic deprivation of sleep alters those very hormones that affect appetite and promotes weight gain. Healthy immune function and the ability to fight off infections and avoid diseases are altered in a sleep-deprived individual. Lack of sleep or drowsiness has been attributed to making mistakes, lapses in judgment, falls, and other accidents. Sleepiness makes one less patient, more irritable, and less energetic and also affects concentration and promotes fatigue. Hypertension, heart-rate irregularity, and increased cortisol stress hormone levels are *present in varying degrees* in the sleep-deprived individual.

The division of sleep into cycles consists of eye movements that are rapid (REM) and non-rapid (NREM). These cycles repeat themselves every ninety minutes, for a total of four to five cycles in an eight-hour sleep period, according to the article "What Happens When You Sleep" (n.d.) on the National Sleep Foundation's website. Sleep cycles through periods of light sleep and deep sleep. Tissue repair and growth occur in stages three and four, which are deemed the most restorative and deepest. The restoration of energy also occurs in stages three and four. REM sleep is the time period in which dreams occur, the brain is active, and the brain and body are provided with energy (Ibid). Facemasks are also available to blot out sunlight.

Night-shift workers often sacrifice sleep to attend to other duties. Given the necessity of sleep, accommodating regular sleep time must become a priority. The night-shift worker must plan time for sleep in order to be refreshed, energetic, alert, able to think clearly, and ready for the duties and challenges of the job and life in general.

The Sleep Environment

The night shifter's sleep environment should mimic or simulate the environment and ambiance of sleeping at night. People should sleep in a cold, very dark room. Remember, darkness signals the release of melatonin, and light stops the production of it. Eliminate the glare of sunlight through the windows and LED lights from electronic devices. Covering the LED light with an opaque dark cloth helps to blot out this light because even the tiny lights from electronic devices can disturb sleep as the body cycles through REM and NREM sleep. Blackout curtains are useful to block out sunlight. Not all curtains with the label blackout actually eliminate all the light that shines in through the windows. I bought a weave-pattern curtain with the title blackout. The weave pattern curtain was not effective in blocking out all the daylight from entering the room. I purchased another set of curtains with a solid double panel that was more conducive to producing a dark room, especially since I placed the solid double panel over the weave pattern curtains. I purchased the blackout curtains from Wal-Mart initially online and then at my local Wal-Mart store. Read the package content carefully. Each package only contains one panel, although there is a picture on the package of two curtains.

Promote a quiet environment. Use white noise, a fan, or recordings of nature or soft music to promote a quiet environment and block out daytime sounds. Earplugs are useful to some, as are face masks. Place cell phones on vibrate or turn the volume to low. Set the thermostat to your comfort level to promote relaxation and to snuggle under the blankets. Some individuals like to read before bedtime. If you read, make sure it's not a stimulating subject. Start calming the mind. Deal with nagging thoughts or a busy mind by writing down thoughts such as schedules, events, and so on in order to avoid trying to remember them later. Play soothing music. Start preparing for sleep on your way home from work. Put on sunshades to start simulating dusk unless you are extremely sleepy. In that case, do what's necessary to maintain wakefulness until you arrive home, or get a ride home to prevent falling asleep at the wheel. Follow your usual bedtime routine. If you take a bath, sprinkle in magnesium salts to further relax the body. Sprinkle lavender and rosemary essential oils on your pillow to breathe in soothing scents to further relax the body.

Your Action Plan—Putting Tools into Action
What is your routine to prepare for sleep?
The objective is to schedule seven or eight hours for deep restful sleep!

1.

2.

3.

4.

5.

6.

Adapting

Night-shift workers should start preparing for their night's work by scheduling time to rest or sleep before the shift begins. To be able to function at night, the shift worker must adapt or slowly move his or her circadian cycle (Price, 2011) to better tolerate working at night and sleeping during the day. I tolerate the night shift if I had a good night's sleep on my day off and proceed to take a nap or rest time before my night shift begins. I work three night shifts per week, so I have four nights to sleep on a regular schedule. It is not uncommon for people to remain on a nocturnal schedule of sleeping during the day and wakefulness at night or sleep part of the night and the morning after even on scheduled days off. Each individual must find his or her balance to maintain his or her circadian clock.

Night shifters often use coffee or other caffeinated drinks to stay awake at night and sedatives to sleep during the day. I was only able to use coffee for the first few years of working at night. I loved my mug of coffee when I worked nights—until I developed cardiac problems as a result of caffeine sensitivity. I had to forget about that cup of coffee or any caffeinated drink, so I learned to use alternative measures. I use ginseng liquid and B-stress vitamins to supply the energy I need. Be careful when selecting energy drinks. A lot of these drinks contain caffeine, which can cause some jitteriness.

How to Stay Awake Without Ruining Your Ability to Sleep

1. Sleep the night before. Rest well before starting the night shift.
2. Consider taking vitamin supplements, especially for energy, alertness, and stamina. Consider B-stress vitamin preparations.
3. Maintain hydration and avoid dehydration.
4. Maintain an exercise regimen for increased energy and for good restful sleep.
5. Consider taking liquid ginseng as needed but not after 3:00 a.m. to prevent interference with sleep when ready to sleep after the night shift.
6. During your shift keep your mind busy. Avoid physical exhaustion. Assist coworkers as needed. Play lively music at a reasonable decibel approved by management.
7. A steady, good, interesting conversation keeps interest high and sleepiness at bay.
8. Consume small healthy meals. Avoid high carbohydrate intake, which has a sedating effect. Heavy meals are weighty in the stomach and promote sleepiness.
9. Have adequate lighting during your shift, and then dim the lights at the end of your shift.
10. Toward the end of the shift, start winding down. Make sure all aspects of your job are completed to ensure a calm quiet mind and smooth transition from one shift to the other.

What works for you to help you stay awake?
Your Action Plan—Putting Tools into Action

1.

2.

3.

4.

5.

6.

.

Sleep Aids

For years after working the night shift, I had no trouble sleeping. Initially I worked 11:00 p.m. to 7:00 a.m. Eight-hour shifts were not hard. I had time to get the children off to school, go to sleep, pick them up, help with homework, and take a two- to three-hour nap before returning for another night shift. In addition, I was able to sleep in the evening when it was dark or at night. I was able to sleep well even during the day. My next job required working three to four twelve-hour shifts per week, which is harder on the body. Unless I am scheduled off, no nap during the early night hours is possible. After two decades of night-shift work, I started having periodic episodes of trouble sleeping. I even had one or two episodes of insomnia.

Different levels of sleeplessness require diverse measures to promote sleep. When I had mild sleeplessness, a hot bath with Epsom salts and lavender essential oil helped to relax me, along with a cup of warm milk. Moderate sleeplessness required over-the-counter sleep aids in addition to the mild sleeplessness remedy. Sleep aids are available from health food stores and local grocery stores. Be careful: some sleep aids, though effective, may leave you feeling hung over or with mild headaches. Episodes of extreme trouble falling asleep require the temporary use of a prescription sleep aid. I consulted with my primary care physician, who prescribed the low dose of five milligrams of Ambien. Sometimes I only needed half of that. Know the side effects of over-the-counter and prescription sleep aids. Do not combine different sleep aids. Plan at least eight hours of sleep to prevent feeling hung over or drowsy upon awakening. I did not want to become dependent on prescription sleep medication, so I weaned myself off and researched information on sleep, the body's need for sleep, natural foods and drinks that increase the body's level of tryptophan, serotonin, and melatonin.

One fruit juice to consider as a choice for melatonin is tart cherry juice. Cherries have many health benefits, including antioxidant, anti-inflammatory, potentially anticarcinogenic, and cardiovascular-protective properties. In addition, cherries also contain melatonin, which promotes sleep (McCune, Kubota, Stendell-Hollis, & Thomson, 2011). The regular consumption of tart cherry juice is an additional measure that is beneficial to night-shift workers. Just one ounce (30cc) provides melatonin in the amount of 85 mcg/day (Turner, 2013). *See also Schor, 2012 and Howatson, et al, 2011 for interesting information regarding cherry juice.* Tart cherry juice remains a primary drink as an adjunct in my routine in preparation for sleep. Night-shift workers must pay attention to food sources that provide melatonin, tryptophan, and serotonin to augment the body's ability to promote sleep. The concentrated tart cherry juice often is stocked at local health stores or the nearest Whole Foods Market.

Nutritional Needs of the
Night-Shift Worker

The night-shift worker has the added stress of working counter to the natural circadian cycle. The night shifter needs the maximum of what the day shift's nutritional needs are plus the benefit of supplementation to supply his or her body with the essential minerals and vitamins depleted by stressors of working at night. Supplementation provided my body with what was needed to maintain and improve energy levels, stamina, and alertness.

After years of working the night shift, I developed fatigue and low energy levels. After ensuring that I had no medical problems that could contribute to the fatigue and low energy levels, I evaluated my diet. I made dietary changes as needed first, and then I looked into vitamin and mineral supplementation. There are many brands of B vitamins. Look particularly for B vitamins with the label Stress B-complex, which supplies all eight of the B vitamins. All of the B vitamins work synergistically to assist our body to function optimally. Whether it's fuel conversion from our foods, helping us stay energized, playing a major role in mood and sleep patterns, helping the body produce serotonin and melatonin, or preventing memory loss—all are essential adjuncts for the night shifter (McDermott, 2014). It is evident that a deficiency of any of these essential vitamins can enhance fatigue, trouble sleeping, and other symptoms night shifters encounter.

Vitamin D, in addition to calcium and phosphorous absorption, functions to enable our immune system to help us resist infections and diseases. Vitamin D is called the sunshine vitamin because sunlight exposure facilitates our body's production of vitamin D. Ten minutes of daily sun exposure constitutes the easiest method to assist the body to produce vitamin D. Also, certain fortified foods and supplements provide vitamin D (Healthline Editorial Team, 2013). Night shifters often are asleep during sunlight hours. The practice of sitting on the patio before and after sleep time can help the night shifter obtain sunlight exposure and relaxation. Consuming food fortified with vitamin D or vitamin D supplements provides some vitamin D, but there is nothing like a little sunlight.

Balanced Healthy Meals and Eating Light at Night

Often night shifters' eating habits mimic the eating habits of daytime workers, which can consist of consuming full meals and simple carbohydrate intake such as candy, cake, and other sweet stuff. Eating donuts provides a sugar rush and quick energy, but results in low energy levels later. Simple carbohydrates interfere with prolonged sleep and over time promote weight gain.

Balanced healthy meals—with complex carbohydrates, lean protein, healthy fats, and fruits and vegetables—are essential elements to maintain health and vitality. Healthy balanced nutritious meals are essential to maintaining internal balance. Healthy balanced meals also supply needed vitamins and minerals and help the body to fight off illness, especially while working at night.

After consuming regular meals of complex carbohydrates, proteins, and fats, digestion can take two to four hours. The total digestive process from ingestion to elimination takes twenty-four to seventy-two hours (Nall, 2013). Medications, emotions, and aging have an effect on the transit time of what we have eaten. In addition, night-shift workers are faced with alterations in the hormones leptin and ghrelin, which play a role in our feeling of fullness and hunger

(Burron, 2014). When sleep-deprived, we feel the need to eat more, which can lead to weight gain.

As we get older, our ability to produce digestive enzymes may be reduced. The lack of digestive enzymes interferes with our body's ability to digest food properly. Replacing digestive enzymes may become necessary. Listen to your body. If you find you are having trouble losing weight, your food is not settling right, or you are feeling bloated and weighed down, then consider the need for digestive enzymes and probiotic supplementation.

Eating lightly at night actually helped to keep my energy level up and prevent undue sleepiness. For the first couple of years, if I did not get a chance to eat before my shift began, then I would eat supper when I could take my break. The heavy meal resulted in sleepiness. I had to walk around or drink coffee to stay awake. I adopted the habit of eating some, if not all, of my supper before going to work and the remainder of my supper and a salad during the night. This habit provided the fuel and nutrients I needed to keep me going without being hungry or fatigued.

The proper balance of bacteria in the intestinal tract is needed for optimal digestion. According to the article "The Science of Probiotics, 2006, on the American Nutrition Association website, the healthy intestinal gut flora consists of a balance of 85 percent good bacteria and 15 percent bad bacteria. Antibiotics, processed foods, sugar, tension, and anxiety can upset this delicate balance.

Probiotics are needed as we age because the bacteria count decreases with aging. Beneficial immune responses are triggered by friendly bacteria in the gut; these immune responses are triggered throughout the body and affect signals generated within the nervous system and the brain (Ibid).

Probiotics can be obtained from fermented foods and beverages, which can be made from starter kits or bought from health food stores. Examples of probiotics that I have noticed in the local Whole Foods store consist of kimchi, sauerkraut, tempeh, fermented soy sauce, kombucha, and kefir. I have tried the kimchi, kombucha, and kefir. Tempeh has a bland taste that takes on the flavor of whatever you cook it with. Kimchi has a very strong cooked cabbaged odor. My favorites are the kombucha and kefir. Kombucha tastes like a fizzy drink in different flavors. Kefir has a smoothie-like yogurt taste. Probiotics are also available in capsule form at many health food stores.

What are your meal/nutritional plans?
Your Action Plan—Putting Tools into Action

1.

2.

3.

4.

5.

6.

7.

8.

9.

10.

Maintaining Energy Balance

Our cells are nourished and receive energy from the food we eat. Literally what's on the end of our fork determines our state of health. Our cells from our brain to our toes and everywhere in between are manufactured/replaced on a regular basis. Enzymes, nutrients, and the energy of fruits and vegetables or lack thereof determine how healthy or unhealthy we are, how quickly we think and process the information in our brain, and the health of our nerves and digestive, skin, and muscular systems, as well as our strength and endurance.

It is interesting to note that raw, natural foods supply the body with the most energy and nutrients. Processed foods and a predominance of our Western diet supplies our body with very little energy and in large amounts can deprive our cells of nutrients and energy. We need to increase our intake of fresh fruits and veggies, especially green veggies, and eat a rainbow of fruits and veggies daily to keep our cells healthy and functioning at optimal or high energy levels. Raw foods and their living enzymes also aid digestion.

God's chemical laboratory in each of us uses the nutrients, enzymes, and other components of plants to generate the energy needed by our cells and for our survival. What happens when our energy levels go below optimum levels? We tend to feel run-down, our organs don't function well, we feel sluggish, and over time toxins build up.

Maintaining hydration is of the utmost necessity. Drinking enough fluid to keep urine a pale yellow color is key to maintaining hydration, a youthful look, and preventing constipation. Keep in mind that coffee and teas have a diuretic effect on the body, so extra fluid is needed to maintain that pale yellow color of urine.

How will you nutritionally maintain your energy level?
Your Action Plan—Putting Tools into Action

1.

2.

3.

4.

5.

6.

7.

8.

9.

10.

Dietary Sources of Tryptophan, Serotonin, and Melatonin

Tryptophan, serotonin, and melatonin are important elements to promote sleep. The connection between tryptophan, serotonin and melatonin is as follows. "Tryptophan is needed by the body to produce serotonin. Serotonin is used to make melatonin...." Zamosky, (n.d.). Tryptophan is an amino acid derived from protein. Turkey is a familiar source of tryptophan. Other sources include poultry, meat, cheese, fish, and eggs.(lbid). The B vitamin, niacin, is produced by the body from tryptophan. Nerves, skin, digestion, and serotonin production are influenced by niacin (Ibid.) The brain chemical serotonin, "plays a large role in mood, and can help to create a feeling of well-being and relaxation" (Ibid.) and better sleep. Couple the protein with a little carbohydrate to elevate serotonin levels in the brain (Ibid.). Some examples according to Dagnelli, n.d. include:

- Chicken or egg salad with shredded or sliced cheese.
- Grilled or baked fish with a little pasta
- Cheesy omelet

Fruits, grains, meat, and vegetables contain the hormone melatonin in small amounts. According to WebMD.com, levels of melatonin from the pineal gland "begin to rise in the mid-to-late evening, remain high most of the night and then drop in the early morning hours" (WebMD, n.d.). Melatonin dietary sources such as oats, pineapples, oranges, bananas, rice, and barley (Renter, 2013), taken at the end of the shift, and sleeping in a dark environment help the night shifter obtain better, longer sleep.

Supplementation of tryptophan and melatonin are available. Let your doctor know of all supplements taken to rule out medical issues as a cause of insomnia. Sleepiness and grogginess after awakening are among a few side effects of melatonin supplementation if it is taken during the day.

The night shifter can select various sleep-promoting snacks to enhance sleep. Pairing of food sources of melatonin, serotonin, and especially tryptophan benefits the night worker. Examples of such pairings include whole grains such as a bowl of (plain) cereal (I like Cheerios) and skim milk, one ounce of cheese on a slice of apple, scrambled egg (I like a boiled egg), low-fat milk or cheese, yogurt with added cherries, or a peanut butter sandwich (try one slice of bread with sugarless peanut butter; I prefer almond butter) (Travis, n.d.).

What is your plan regarding maintaining your tryptophan,
serotonin, and melatonin levels?
Your Action Plan—Putting Tools into Action

1.

2.

3.

4.

5.

6.

7.

8.

9.

10.

Night-Shift Work and Family Life

worked the night shift from the time my children were infants through most of their high school years. Initially I only worked 11:00 p.m. to 7:00 a.m., which was not as stressful on the body as working 7:00 p.m. to 7:00 a.m. I worked the night shift to be available in case I was needed by my family during the day. Most of the time I was able to sleep at least seven hours, but sometimes I was needed to pick up a sick child. I liked the fact that I was able to see the children off to school and pick them up afterward. I was able to help with homework and then get a nap in the evening before I went back to work. My husband would help with homework if he got off work early enough.

Planning family time and togetherness was important to stay connected. If my husband and I did not talk face-to-face, then we communicated by phone or left messages. Coordinating everyone's schedule was essential to maintaining order and meeting appointments. I can honestly say at times I did not get as much sleep as needed, and I felt better if I was able to sleep extra on the days I was off from work. The children learned to be quiet when Mommy was sleeping, as my husband supervised and cared for them during the times I had to work. On my weekend off, they were rewarded with favorite activities: going to the movies or park, renting movies, having friends over, and so on. Having a babysitter provided time for my husband and I to have a date night periodically.

Maintaining as much normalcy to family life as possible was important. Going to school functions, field trips, and parent-teacher conferences was important, and by working the night shift, I was able to attend most of these events.

I would suggest that you schedule your sleep time as you would schedule an important appointment. Make it a priority to sleep as much as you can after your shift, and then take a nap or rest period before the next shift. A parent who is rested is much more attentive to the needs of the family.

Creating a Healthy Balance at Home

Let family and friends know when it is OK to call. Open communications with family and friends, and let them know and make sure they understand your schedule. Communicate in person or via notes, e-mails, texts, phone calls, and Post-it notes. Schedule a date night and family time, and connect with family and friends when not working.

Educate family and friends about the risks of night-shift work, how you are adapting, and the plans you have put in place to accommodate the needs of your family and friends. As stated before, night-shift workers often sacrifice sleep time to attend to family affairs. Come to an agreement between spouses/partners on amicable ways to attend to the children and family needs and provide ways for the night shifter to obtain the amount of sleep needed.

Maintain as much normalcy to family life as possible. If spouses work opposing shifts, plan a date night, family time, and get-togethers. Communicate face-to-face, by phone and e-mails, and use whatever technology is available to enhance communication. Say good night or good morning to the family using Skype. Leave notes or phone messages. Teach the children when it is OK to wake Mom or Dad and how to play quietly. Reward cooperation with treats and movies, and value family time.

Let family and friends know when you are scheduled to work, your off days, and when it is OK to call or come by. Post a sign on the front door to politely let unexpected visitors or vendors know you are sleeping and to return at a set time.

Stress Management

Night-shift work puts added stress on the body by working counter to the usual circadian cycle of wakefulness during the day and sleep at night. One of the hormones the body releases in response to stress is cortisol. "Overexposure to cortisol and other stress hormones can disrupt almost all bodily processes and can lead to anxiety, depression, digestive problems, heart disease, sleep problems, weight gain, memory and concentration impairment" (Mayo Clinic Staff, 2013, para. 8).

It is essential, especially for the night-shift worker, to learn healthy ways to cope with the stressors of night shifts and life in general. After work some individuals get together for drinks, especially after a stressful shift. A nightcap helps with stress relief, especially when coworkers get together and vent. However, alcohol is a double-edged sword; it initially promotes sleep, but the body becomes used to it, and prolonged use actually interferes with restful sleep (Roehrs & Roth, n.d.). In addition, driving while under the influence of alcohol is illegal and dangerous. The selection of a designated driver would solve this problem. The development of alternate stress management techniques should be explored.

Two tools of stress management are monitoring stress levels and reactions to life stressors. Have a plan in place to manage stress. My stress management tools include scheduling massages on a regular basis, exercises using strength training and cardio exercises at least three times a week, yoga, deep breathing, getting enough sleep, warm or hot baths, diversionary activities (make time for fun), and healthy balanced meals. Sometimes it's best to talk things out or vent with coworkers, family, and/or close friends. Deep breathing, tai chi, recreational sports, and routinely getting together with friends for laughs and fun are also good stress relievers.

One of my favorite mantras that I adopted from someone is *it is what it is*. Develop a mind-set of approaching work that consists of saying *I only have twelve hours to work; I am not going to let this event or shift upset me or get the best of me. I will do what needs to be done, and then I am out of here!* Make a decision of what your reaction is going to be, and then develop a certain mind-set to not let the stress get to you. In the past I handled stress by fussing and complaining as others do. A new *saying* of mine is *Life happens—do what you can and move on*, don't waste time and energy. Remain positive and self-affirming.

Most, if not all, corporations have debriefing sessions or Employee Assistance Programs (EAP) available when the worker encounters traumatizing events, such as the death of a patient or client. When police, firefighters, and emergency medical technicians/services are called to the scene of an accident or shooting, debriefing or use of the Employee Assistance Program (EAP) afterward allows for venting of feelings, emotions, and frustrations. Bottling up, internalizing, or becoming jaded results in unresolved stress, health problems, negative attitudes, and negative actions.

Promote a peaceful mind through meditation, adhering to your religious practices, and self-care activities such as obtaining massages and exercising. Meditation quiets the mind, allows focused attention, and moderates the stress response. Adhering to one's religious practices develops compassion, inner strength, positive attitudes, and the ability to quickly forgive perceived or actual wrongs.

Stress can manifest itself in the body in the form of knots in the muscles and stiffness. Massages became a necessity for me to obtain relief from knots in muscles and promote circulation and relaxation of tight muscles. Exercise promotes circulation to the body and brain, strengthens muscles, creates more alertness, and is a natural stress reliever. Stretch before and after exercising to improve flexibility. Yoga promotes flexibility and improves the body's response to stress. See Appendix 5 and 6 for information on deep breathing, stretching, and flexibility.

General recommendations regarding exercise include avoiding exercise activities at least three hours before bedtime to prevent interference with the ability to fall asleep. Exercise, if possible, before the night shift to increase energy levels and alertness.

What is your action plan to deal with the stressors of the night shift?
Your Action Plan—Putting Tools into Action

1.

2.

3.

4.

5.

Corporate Measures to Assist in the Health Maintenance of Night-Shift Workers

I think managers should have to work at least one night shift to understand what the night-shift worker goes through. The old adage of *one should walk a mile in another's shoes* is quite appropriate.

Night-shift workers should communicate to management what shifts are more compatible for them and whether or not the shift will interfere with or run counter to the shift of their spouses. Most management teams will try to schedule workers with shifts that are compatible with their spouses. Management also often permits workers to switch schedules among one another to accommodate their needs.

Corporations should invest in measures to assist in the health maintenance of night-shift workers. Employers need to become aware of the risks of working the night shift. Shift differentials, though beneficial, seem insufficient as the only compensation for the night-shift worker. Companies that invest in health and wellness packages in addition to the regular health insurances encourage and advocate health for their employees. Additionally, companies that develop health and wellness packages for night-shift workers place the night-shift worker on a path to ensure his or her health while addressing the risks of night-shift work. These health and wellness packages should include education regarding the risks of night-shift work, adapting to the night shift, measures to address the risks of night-shift work, adjusting the circadian cycle, nutritional and conventional means to promote sleep, the importance of sleep, stress management, and maintaining a balance at work and within the family.

Employers and managers need to understand that night-shift workers, like day shifters, require eight hours of sleep to function optimally. Meetings should be scheduled at an amicable time for both day and night shifts. A shift beginning at 5:30 p.m. to the night shifter is the same as 5:30 a.m. to the day shifter. Companies should rotate scheduled meetings to alternate between night shift and day shift.

Managers should assign shift work in blocks that allow workers time to adjust to the night shift and enough time to recuperate on days off. Workers who rotate day and night shifts have a harder time adjusting their circadian cycles. Lack of adequate sleep time, affects the worker who rotates day and night shifts, particularly in a one-week period. Adequate time off to adjust between the two shifts provides the individual who rotates shifts time to adjust his or her circadian cycle and receive adequate sleep time and quality. It is recommended to schedule shifts in biweekly blocks before rotating to the alternate shifts. Scheduling in increments of day-shift blocks, evening-shift blocks, and then night-shift blocks allows for the worker to acclimate to these different shifts and adjust his or her circadian cycle slowly and appropriately (Smith and Eastman, 2012).

Periodically it may be necessary for the night-shift worker to come off the night shift if lack of sleep interferes with job performance, the health of the night-shift worker, or family dynamics.

Corporations, organizations, and companies may want to consider dimming lights for night-shift workers. The regular use of fluorescent lights in the workplace is common. Although bright lights enhance the workplace environment and permit more light entry into the eyes, night-shift workers may benefit from dimming the lights to acceptable levels that do not interfere with work performance and yet allow for less light entry into the eyes, thus permitting less suppression of melatonin. Patients in hospitals also benefit from having lights dimmed at night as health-care professionals provide care ordered by physicians.

What measures have your managers/supervisors implemented to assist the night-shift workers?

1.

2.

3.

4.

5.

6.

7.

8.

9.

10.

In Summary—Strategies for Health and Wellness

K now the risks of night-shift work.
Know how to plan your health care to reduce the risks of night-shift work.
Consume nutritious food and beverages.
Maintain hydration.
Maintain a healthy weight or lose weight.
Prioritize and plot out your sleep time.
Use sleep aids judiciously as needed.
Create an environment that induces sleep.
Plan self-care activities and family fun times.
Adopt healthy stress management regimens.
Invest in massages and/or plan a couples' massage day.
Enjoy life and adopt an attitude of gratitude and thankfulness.

Conclusions

Millions of Americans work nights and in doing so inherently expose themselves to the risks of altering their circadian cycle. Knowledge is power! Once you understand the circadian cycle (chapter 4) and have learned the risks of working night-shift spoken of in chapter 5, then you will understand why you should take the steps outlined in chapters 6-9 to enable you to fall asleep easily and obtain good-quality sleep. Good quality sleep is essential to maintain alertness and professional performance of work requirements. In chapter 10-12 you learned about the nutritional needs of the night-shift worker, how to maintain energy balance, and what foods to incorporate into your diet to promote a healthy work-sleep balance. Ideas were given on how to balance your work and your family/ home, as well as stress management tips that will help in all facets of life. Family measures to adapt and prioritize sleep and maintain balance alleviate some of the external pressures of working the night shift. Finally, chapter 15 indicates steps your employer could take to promote good health for night-shift workers. Corporate measures to assist the night-shift worker to maintain health and wellness ensure a healthy employee who will remain with the company longer than someone whose employer does not.

The appendixes provide adjunct information regarding weight loss, how to make the body inhospitable to cancer, detoxification, exercise, flexibility, and the Meridian Assessment tool to enhance the employees endeavors for health and wellness. Information on health coaching, it's purpose and benefits provide a resource to assist night shift workers.

Appendix 1
Weight Loss

t is possible to lose weight while working the night shift. One must be determined, committed, and have a mind-set to return to an ideal weight and become healthier. Otherwise shift work compounds the health problems of obesity. As mentioned earlier, sleep deprivation or an inadequate amount and quality of sleep opens the door for hypertension and other health conditions, in addition to elevated cortisol levels from chronic sleep loss. Elevated evening cortisol levels are "likely to promote the development of insulin resistance, a risk factor for obesity and diabetes" (Van Caute, Knutson, Leproult, & Spiegel, 2005). Addressing one's sleep needs and preventing sleep deprivation constitute a major hurdle in one's endeavor to lose weight. In fact, "getting fewer than six hours of sleep a night is linked with increases in the hunger-stimulating hormone ghrelin, decrease in insulin sensitivity (a risk factor for diabetes) and decreases in the hormone leptin (which is key for energy balance and food intake)" (Huffington Post, 2012). You should aim for eight hours of sleep. Once rested, the motivation and the drive to achieve one's weight loss goals become achievable.

Over my two and a half decades of working the night shift, I have lost over twenty pounds twice. In my late twenties to age thirty, weight loss endeavors were easier. It only took four to six months to lose twenty pounds by eliminating simple carbohydrates, exercising three to four times a week, maintaining hydration, and incorporating lots of fresh fruits, vegetables, and lean proteins into my diet. In my forties, weight loss endeavors took nearly one year to return me to my appropriate weight for my height. In my fifties, I took online classes to obtain my Bachelor of Science degree in nursing and continued working the night shift. I did not have much opportunity to exercise, and in addition, going through menopause resulted in me gaining thirty pounds. I had to double my efforts at exercising, ensure that I was not chronically sleep deprived, and investigate why I became bloated and had other digestive issues when I ate grain sources of carbohydrates. I incorporated lots of green vegetables for energy, a rainbow of fruits and vegetables, and lean protein. I achieved my weight loss goal of thirty pounds in one year.

Changes in carbohydrate metabolism, excess calorie intake, heavy meals, quick and ready access to simple carbohydrates, lack of exercise, and lack of sleep promote weight gain in night-shift workers. Addressing these causative factors can curb the propensity to gain weight and start the night-shift worker on the road to weight loss. Changes in carbohydrate metabolism can manifest themselves as bloating, gas, changes in bowel pattern, and weight gain. The body is having difficulty processing the carbohydrates. Among my strategies I sought medical help to confirm I did not have any other medical condition. Then I decided to investigate. I suggest a starting point is to begin recording what foods you consume that cause uncomfortable symptoms and eliminate them from your diet for a few weeks. Then, add the food items back into your diet slowly, one at a time. If the symptoms reoccur, it means that your body has trouble processing that food. In my late forties and now fifties, I limit the amount of carbohydrates from grain sources, and I take enzymes to help my body process or break down the carbohydrates I consume. "Enzymes are complex proteins that cause a specific chemical change in all parts of the body. For example, they can help breakdown the foods we eat so the body can use them" (Enzyme, 2013, p. 1).

Keep track of your caloric intake. Heavy meals are usually laden with calories. Even healthy meals using healthy fats should consist of modest amounts of oil. Simple carbohydrates such as cookies and cake are your nemesis and supply extra calories. Eating late at night supplies food at a time when the digestive processes have slowed down. To lose one pound of fat, one must burn or eliminate thirty-five hundred calories.

Lack of sleep leaves one fatigued and feeling drained, which results in a lack of motivation to exercise unless one has a mind-set to lose weight and become healthier. The motivating behavioral change to increase physical activity often comes about as dissatisfaction with one's look, the way clothes fit, lack of energy and endurance, being tired of feeling heavy, and having body aches and pain. A strong factor also is a desire to address medical problems inherent with weight gain. "For every pound of weight gained adds four pounds of pressure on your knees as each step is taken whereas modest weight loss lightens the load on your joints" (Warner, 2005).

Let's start with ensuring adequate sleep to boost energy, lower cortisol levels, and lower the tendency for insulin resistance related to inadequate sleep. Check with your primary care physician to rule out any factors that may preclude exercising. If coming from a sedentary lifestyle, start with walking and progress to more vigorous forms of exercise as endurance and tolerance dictate. Other strategies include:

- Allocate time to exercise to build strength, endurance, and flexibility.
- Build core muscles to strengthen the abdominal muscles and back muscles.
- Incorporate stretching and exercises to improve flexibility to improve posture and joint movement.
- Strive to exercise five to six days per week.
- Exercise a minimum of thirty minutes per day or 180 minutes per week.
- Strive to exercise hard enough to generate sweat and work muscles.
- If funds permit, join group exercise classes such as Yoga®, Pilates®, Jazzercise®, or Zumba®, or go online and access your desired type of exercises.

- Consider hiring a personal trainer, at least for a short period of time.
- In your endeavors to lose weight, do not reduce your caloric intake below twelve hundred calories per day. Reduction of daily caloric intake below twelve hundred prompts the body to save or store calories instead of burning calories.
- If you have difficulty counting calories, I suggest counting carbohydrates. According to the primal diet plan to promote weight loss, "maintain carbohydrate intake between 50 and 100 grams/day" (Sisson, 2012).

Appendix 2
Strategies for Effective Weight Loss

Effective weight loss begins with a desire for a change and a plan to implement change.
Record and post your commitment, intentions, and goals **for weight loss to re**new and affirm your goals daily, and then **p**ost the typed or handwritten goals, commitment, and intentions in several visible places that you feel comfortable with. Seek peace and joy as you attend to your daily activities. Plan self-care days for yourself.

Set aside time daily to plan healthy meal preparation and cooking. One of the principles of the Institute for Integrative Nutrition (IIN)® is to cook once and eat two to three times. (IIN is the health coaching program I attended and where I obtained my certification.) One day you may cook more than one protein. Another day you may have time to cook several vegetables, some to eat for the day and the rest to freeze or eat on another day. Maintain hydration. Dehydration can be confused with hunger. Before reaching for food, try a glass of water, coconut water, clear Gatorade, or flavored water with real fruit such as blueberries, strawberries, limes, cherries, or celery. Incorporate a salad with lunch and dinner. Another principle of IIN is the 90/10 rule: 90 percent of the time plan to eat healthy, and allow 10 percent of the time for those times when healthy cooking may not be possible or if someone at home or work brings in sweets.

Cravings can sometimes sideline progress toward weight loss. Differentiate between cravings and a desire for a particular food that someone near you is consuming. At times family members or coworkers may be eating some snack such as chips or pretzels. If offered and you desire some, have a few (not the whole bag) and go on with your day. Just count that as part of your 10 percent cheat time. If you have a yearning for some particular type of food item, take the time to stop and consider whether perhaps your body may be trying to tell you of a particular need. When working at night if you are getting sleepy, you may find yourself seeking food to keep you awake. Your need is sleep, but if punching out and taking a twenty-minute nap is not feasible, then try going for a walk or striking up a lively conversation instead of eating simple carbohydrates such as cake, cookies, and candy. Address your sleep needs after work and take a nap before your next shift. Make a fruit salad and bring some to work, or add fruit such as strawberries, blueberries, and dried cranberries to salads to add that sweet taste and satisfy a sweet tooth. Bring sweet vegetables such as sweet potato slices or carrots with raspberry dressing as part of your meal to work. Graze or have several small healthy meals throughout the shift to stave off hunger and low blood sugar. Ensure nutritious meals with a variety of vegetables to avoid cravings such as those for salty foods, which are due to nutritional deficits. Greens and a variety of fruits and vegetables supply the vitamins and minerals needed by the body. Consume a balance of nutrient-dense foods and adequate low-fat protein, complex carbohydrates, and healthy fats such as olive oil. Suggestions such as

- Fresh fruit salad,
- Mixed green salad (romaine lettuce, watercress, kale, spinach, arugula) with a variety of vegetables such as tomatoes, carrots, squash, zucchini, radish, sprinkled with dried cranberries, whole wheat or gluten free pasta
- Grilled chicken, fish, or turkey.

- Home made vinaigrette dressing with olive or avocado oil and and balsamic vinegar

Other types of cravings may consist of an emotional or spiritual need. Emotional eating can result from being bored, dissatisfied with a relationship or job, or stressed out. Sometimes you just need a hug or someone to validate you or say you are loved or appreciated. Lack of spiritual practice and/or meditation contributes to consuming empty calories or mindless eating. Take some time to sit and reflect. Talking to a trusted friend or professional about what is actually going on mentally, physically, or spiritually can yield some answers.

Ensure a bowel movement at least daily. If your fiber intake is adequate, then more frequent bowel movements result, as the transit time through the intestines is increased to clear the contents and prevent reabsorption of toxins or other harmful substances your body is in the process of clearing out. Reward yourself when you reach milestones or goals. Rewards should include primarily non-food items, such as jewelry, facials, time out for fun, a new scarf, and so on.

Things that can affect our digestive process include constipation, medications, inactivity, and diseases, which can result in slowing or altering of digestion. If you are taking medications, read the inserts or go online to view the side effects. Some medications can cause weight gain and possible gastrointestinal side effects such as bloating, diarrhea, and/or constipation. If faced with these and other side effects that prevent weight loss, then schedule an appointment with your physician to address these side effects and change to a medication that does not produce these side effects.

As a health coach, I encourage clients to consider the suggestions below for maintaining their healthy weight:

1. Understand your body and your reasons for weight gain.
2. Stay active, consume more fiber, drink plenty of water, and manage your weight.
3. Receive regular health screenings.

4. Know your family history and plan accordingly to not succumb to familial illnesses or diseases. Fill out the following
form to begin your planning.

Family History: What health conditions run in your family?

Mother_____

Father_____

Grandparents_____

What health conditions are you dealing with?

_____

What health conditions do you plan to no longer have to deal with
once you lose weight and develop a healthier lifestyle?

_____

What strategies do you have for weight loss?
Your Action Plan—Putting Tools into Action

1.

2.

3.

4.

5.

6.

7.

8.

9.

Appendix 3
Forging A Body Inhospitable to Cancer

As night-shift workers, we need to remember that the World Health Organization has indicated that night-shift work is a probable cause for cancer development (Smith & Eastman, 2012). I would be remiss if I did not say that getting off the night shift would be a logical step to take to minimize our potential for succumbing to cancer. If coming off the night shift is not a step you can take at this time, then the information provided in this section can help you shore up or fortify your body to make it inhospitable to cancer. As stated previously, for night-shift workers maintaining melatonin levels remains crucial to moderate the production of estrogen. In addition to adequate quality sleep in a dark environment, night-shift workers can make their body inhospitable to cancer by addressing other areas of life.

Cancer is a disease with many predisposing factors. Environmental toxins, hormonal imbalance, immune system weakness, stress, poor or overly indulgent diets, depression, resentment, and unforgiveness can sicken or weaken the body and allow for cancer to develop and grow. We live in a busy, sometimes crazy, stressful world. The nourishment or lack thereof, lifestyle choices, and our emotional, mental, and spiritual states can either enhance our health or propel us down an unhealthy path. Continual intake of processed foods, sugary foods, and excess protein provide the environment for a weakened impaired immunity, which allows cancer cells to thrive and grow.

We have an arsenal of defensive strategies to shore up our bodies and make them inhospitable to cancer. This arsenal includes:

- An intake of a variety of fruits and vegetables that keep our cells in an immune-supportive environment.
- Stress management to avoid the continual production of cortisol in response to stress. I once heard that stress is 10 percent event and 90 percent our reaction to the stress.
- Discipline in mental and emotional response to stress is critical.
- Our level of spiritual health. Resentment and unforgiveness flood the body with chemicals that eventually harm the individual holding onto these emotions. Someone once said that refusing to forgive someone is compared to someone taking poison and expecting the other person to die. Unforgiveness poisons the very individual who holds it in his or her heart. A long time ago, I had unforgiveness for someone who did something to me in my childhood. That unforgiveness became such a heavy burden on my heart and shoulders that I asked God to give me the will to want to forgive the individual who had wronged me. Eventually I was able to forgive, had the burden lifted, and was able to go on with life. Life has enough struggles and challenges without adding the burden of unforgiveness.

Our arsenal of blood-purifying food with cancer-fighting nutrients includes garlic, organic scallion onions, leeks, shallots, and chive herbs (National Cancer Institute, n.d.). Watercress and other cruciferous greens contain nutrient-rich components that can assist our immune system (Ibid).

According to the article, "Healing Properties of Watercress", Hippocrates, the father of Western medicine, referred to watercress as the "cure among cures...and is high in Vitamin C, beta-carotene, and lutein...and researchers have found daily consumption of watercress to reduce DNA damage in blood cells. DNA damage in blood cells is an indicator of a person's overall cancer risk."(Heal With Food, n.d., para. 1,2,3). Most local supermarkets stock this cruciferous green vegetable, and gardening in moist warm soil can yield an abundant crop if you choose to grow it at home.

Leafy dark green vegetables fortify and are essential to the building and maintenance of a healthy immune system and body. When you nourish yourself with greens, you may naturally crowd out the foods that make you sick. Eat your salads with plenty of dark green leafy vegetables, or incorporate dark green leafy vegetables as side dishes with lean protein.

Cut out the high intake of empty calories and sucrose. Aranceta and Perez-Rodrigo (2013) report that there is "possible evidence of a positive association between glycemic index and colorectal cancer." (Para.3). Weight gain and subsequent obesity are risk factors in the development of cancer. Read food labels to identify hidden sugar or glucose. Look for key words such as fructose, lactose, sucrose, and so on. Choose nutritious naturally sweet treats to be eaten in moderation. Scientifically it is uncertain whether artificial sweeteners cause cancer, but there is some cause for concern when a sweetener was manufactured initially for the purpose of use as a pesticide or when cancer results in lab animals that are given such sweeteners. Better choices are to stick to natural forms of sugar such as honey, agave nectar, molasses, and maple syrup. These natural sweeteners have protecting antioxidant and nutrient factors. Why choose empty calories when you can have sweetness with the beneficial antioxidant properties? Stevia is a plant source of a sweetener that does not have any clinical evidence of cancer risk or cancer-promoting factors. The American Heart Association reports that women should not consume more than six teaspoonfuls of sugar per day and that men should not consume more than nine teaspoons per day (n.d.).

If you have a family history of cancer, you should view processed foods and sugar as undesirable. I have heard some people say the prevalence of sweets or other unhealthy foods and drinks is so great, why should they try to eat healthy? These individuals are justifying unhealthy behavior. My preference is not to die of any diseases, especially cancer or any complications related to obesity. I prefer to go quietly in my bed. I have seen the suffering of those who did not take care of their health. It is just too much of an impact physically, emotionally, psychologically, economically, and financially on the individual, family, community, and public. It's not worth the momentary pleasure that leads to lifelong illness or diseases. Our taste buds have been trained to like artificial or unhealthy foods and liquids. Give your body a chance to come to love the taste of natural fresh foods, such as fruits, vegetables, whole grains, lean meat, and healthy fats. An occasional sweet treat 10 percent of the time is acceptable as opposed to daily. I guarantee if you put cranberries, strawberries, and other suitable fruits in salads, this will moderate or satisfy a sweet tooth and also help to limit the amount of pastries consumed. My philosophy is to consume fewer nonnutritive calories, which equals less weight gain. A healthier body will last longer than a body that is subject to unhealthy meals and lifestyles.

Appendix 4

Additional Tools to Forge a Body Inhospitable to Cancer

Detoxification consists of ridding the body of chemical toxins exposed to in food and in everyday living. Many thousands of chemicals are allowed by the United States to be made and used in our everyday products. Detoxification helps to unclog our elimination system. One of the many benefits of detoxing includes the ability to "strengthen our body's fight against cancer cells and generate healthy cells" (Danilyan, 2012, p. 1). Detoxing is essential for anyone who wants to continue to make his or her body inhospitable to cancer. Natural food sources that promote detoxification include kale, garlic onion, blueberries, strawberries, collard greens, watercress, broccoli, cabbage, and carrots (Ibid). With these nutritious foods, you can make a powerhouse salad or smoothie to fortify and heal the body.

According to Rosenthal (2007), balance primary and secondary foods to maintain equilibrium in physical, emotional, and psychological health. Primary foods consist of the nonfood aspects of our lives, such as healthy relationships, regular physical activity, a fulfilling career, and spiritual practice (Ibid). Secondary foods consist of the actual food we consume (Ibid).

Help your body not succumb to cancer by avoiding or at least limiting the use of food or liquids in plastic containers. We all know not to leave bottles of water in a hot car because plasticizers can leach into the water. We know not to heat food or liquids in soft plastic containers because chemicals can leach into the food. Plasticizers are chemicals from which plastic bottles are made. Any chemicals you do not expose your body to benefit you. Some of the chemicals utilized in the making of plastic bottles are known hormone disruptors or mimickers of estrogen (Mileva, Baker, Konkle, & Bielajew, 2014).

Today we come in contact with thousands of chemicals. Become knowledgeable and selective in what you allow your body to be exposed to. Reduce the percentage of chemicals you come in contact with. Pour water or other liquids into glass containers. Use filtered water from home and pour that water into glass bottles. Eighty-five percent of the time, I use glass bottles to transport my drinks, water, juice, and other liquids. Any reduction of chemical exposure lessens the possibility of affecting the growing and developing cells of the body. Each person is responsible for his or her own health. I am a minimalist when it comes to food or liquids that I use from plastic containers. The less available chemical that enters my body, the less endocrine or hormonal disruptor chemicals I am exposed to—the fewer things my body has to deal with in its attempt to prevent DNA damage, inflammation, and derangement of cellular development or division.

Prior to implementing my weight loss and health and wellness plan, I felt like my body was inflamed. I had swollen joints, breast tenderness, and lumpy-like areas under my arms and lateral breast areas. By incorporating a detoxification plan to remove any toxins or chemicals my body stored in fat cells, in conjunction with eating healthy meals, I slowly recovered and no longer felt inflamed. Once the body removed any offending elements, circulating in my body or stored in fat cells in my breasts, abdomen, and body, then the swollen joints and tender lumpy breast areas resolved. I drank warm water and lemon juice before meals, ate grapefruit twice daily, and drank plenty of water to flush out my cells and kidneys. I was drinking about sixty-four ounces of water to prevent a sluggish metabolism, prevent dehydration, and assist elimination. The fruits, vegetables, and oatmeal provided enough fiber to increase the number of bowel movements from one to three times per day, which prevented reabsorption of any toxins or chemicals I may have ingested or been exposed to.

Some people don't take the time to make little changes in behavior to make positive changes in their health. Small incremental changes in attitude, selection, and behavior can cumulatively have major benefits in improving health. All it takes is knowledge and determination.

Exercise

General recommendations for exercise include exercising thirty minutes/day for health and wellness benefits. Inadequate amounts of exercise and weight gain are risk factors for cancer development.

Use the football's offensive strategy as you make strides to make your body inhospitable to cancer. Address the risks of night-shift work, consider any genetic factors, and adhere to annual physical exams, wellness checkups, annual mammograms, and lab work. As per physician instructions, women should conduct monthly breast self-examination as recommended. Address any health concerns. Be positive. Strive to have an attitude of gratitude and thankfulness.

In my thirty-one years of nursing (over twenty-five years on the night shift), each of my mammograms has been negative, just showing benign changes in the breast. Now, when I was thirty pounds overweight, I did have lumpy areas in the breast, especially in the areas on the side of the breast, but that resolved with weight loss, getting fit, eliminating pro-inflammatory foods (such as excess meat, and sugary products), and consuming nutritious meals as I incorporated foods with anti-cancer properties. It may have been just inflammatory changes, but that resolved, and my next mammogram test results showed only benign changes.

I now have my best and deepest sleep. My circadian cycle has been adjusted, resulting in my deepest sleep between midnight and 2:00 a.m. I can also sleep well between the hours of 10:00 p.m. to 7:00 a.m. on my days off. My daily stress management includes some form of exercise, deep breathing, monitoring my reaction to stress, participating in my religious practice, listening to uplifting music, and maintaining a positive can-do attitude, with thankfulness and gratitude for each day. I practice self-care and do not feel bad when I treat myself to an occasional sweet treat or a nonfood item/activity. Practice self-care in order for you to care for your family. I participated in Jazzercise®—two or three times per week, Yoga® for twenty minutes two times per week, and stretching exercises daily. Since I have lost weight, my stomach has shrunk. I cannot eat large portion sizes, nor do I have a desire to. Small, frequent, nutritious meals when I am off and at work keep my energy level up. When working the night shift, I include a green smoothie that consists of cranberry juice, a level teaspoon of spirulina and chorella, one scoop of whey protein powder, ginseng liquid (for energy), and one-half packet of Stevia. I sip on the smoothie periodically throughout the night until 3:00 a.m. I wear sunshades on the ride home from work. Upon returning home I drink my cherry-magnesium warm drink in three to four ounces of water, a half cup of chamomile tea, or warm hot cocoa. If hungry I eat a slice of apple with shredded cheese or a little warm oatmeal with almond milk. I listen to relaxing music while preparing for sleep, unplug my landline phone (family and friends have my cell number), put my cell phone on vibrate, and set my alarm if I need to wake up at a certain time in the afternoon. Any pressing or busy thoughts I write down to get the thoughts out of my mind. My room is dark, simulating the night environment. I sprinkle drops of lavender and rosemary on my pillow, breathe deeply, relax, and go into a deep sleep.

What will you implement to make your body inhospitable to cancer?
Your Action Plan—Putting Tools into Action

1.

2.

3.

4.

5.

6.

7.

8.

9.

10.

Appendix 5
Deep Breathing and Stretching Exercises

n our daily routine of activities at home or at work, we often forget about the benefits of periodically taking deep breaths, let alone consciously deciding to practice deep breathing exercises. *Deep breathing* promotes relaxation, combats stress, calms the mind, increases energy, and promotes detoxification via the respiratory system. Deep breathing upon awakening and periodically throughout the day and at night promotes restful sleep. Deep breathing prompts the body to release the natural pain-relieving chemical called endorphin (Tucker, 2014). Dr. Andrew Weil also has a relaxing beneficial deep breathing exercise called the 4-7-8, which is beneficial to individuals who become upset (do it before reacting), have internal tension, have mild to moderate anxiety, or want to sleep better (Weil, 2015). Visit http://www.drweil.com/drw/u/VDR00112/The-4-7-8-Breath-Benefits-and-Demonstration.html for a live demonstration of the 4-7-8 deep breathing technique.

Stretching improves muscle flexibility and loosens tight muscles. Anyone who is faced with prolonged sitting, whether at home or at the office, awakens with stiffness, or experiences muscle tension due to stress should get into the habit of stretching. We are often told to slowly stretch and warm up before exercises and stretch or cool down afterward. Besides loosening tight muscles, stretching provides the added benefit of increased blood flow or circulation to the muscles. I have been told by fitness trainers that stretching should occur without bouncing, in a steady smooth manner without any significant discomfort or pain. If you regularly carry heavy totes or bags, then stretching can relieve sore muscles resulting from the heavy loads. I experienced whiplash from a car accident thirty years ago and still periodically experience muscle tension in my neck and back. If I am stressed, the neck is my first area to experience stiffness or tightness, followed by areas in my back. Stretching exercises help to lessen the muscle tension and stiffness.

My favorite stretching exercises focus attention to the neck and shoulders, back, hips, legs, and feet. For my neck and shoulders, shoulder shrugs followed by relaxing the shoulders, then rolling the shoulders back and down, help. Also, rolling the head slowly side to side is very helpful. For the back I like reaching for the stars one hand at a time while stepping to the same side and pointing the toes. I like stretching the Achilles tendon by stepping on a stool and alternately letting the heels stretch down to the floor. Placing my feet on a yoga block while sitting at the computer allows me to periodically stretch my Achilles tendon effortlessly. My swivel chair affords me the opportunity to stretch side to side while sitting at the computer. View the website **http://physicaltherapy.about.com/od/flexibilityexercises/a/stretchbasics.htm** for helpful safety tips regarding stretching.

Maintain hydration before and after stretching or exercising to allow the body to mobilize and remove toxins or by-products from cells and muscles. Exercise permits the body to remove stored products for elimination from the body via the lymphatic system to be sent to the intestines for defecation, kidneys for urination, skin for sweating, and respiratory systems for exhaling. Slow deep breathing during stretching helps the body eliminate toxins and metabolites from the respiratory system.

Have you ever had neck stiffness, headaches, sore shoulder muscles, tightened stiff back and hip areas, decreased flexibility, decreased joint movements, or bones pulled out of place or rotated because of tight muscles? *I have.* I've had spinal rotation, muscle spasms, and one or the other hip area pulled higher than the other due to tight back muscles. People in stressful jobs, whether these jobs are sedentary or active, experience these occurrences more than others. Physical, psychological, and/or emotional stress results in the body responding by tightening muscles in the neck, shoulders, back, and hips. Knot-like areas can occur under the scapulas, and adhesions between muscles, between muscles and tendons, and between tendons and bones, especially among individuals in high-paced stressful jobs. Muscles shorten, especially in the neck and shoulders, from the body being held in daily tense postures or positions. Chronic muscle tension can progress to knots or trapped pockets of toxin that cause pain and limit mobility. All of these responses can occur in any part of the muscular-skeletal system. Dehydration further magnifies the body's muscular-skeletal response to stress. Finding time to maintain hydration is a challenge during busy work times, but as soon as possible, you should drink water. Health-care facilities do not allow drinking of fluids at the workstation. Stealing away to the break room for a drink of water is a must.

Appendix 6
Exercises That Promote Flexibility

Some exercises in addition to stretching promote flexibility, such as yoga and Pilates. Building core strength and suppleness in addition to flexibility are inherent principles of yoga and Pilates. Yoga, a discipline that involves mental, physical, and spiritual awareness, originated in India. Yoga movements or poses can be used to develop strength, and endurance, improve muscle tone and posture, relieve stress, and increase flexibility (Woodyard, 2011).

Pilates helps the individual develop awareness of his or her body in movement, symmetry, and coordination and development of core strength and control. Regular Pilates practice produces health benefits such as improved balance and posture, core stability and strength, treatment and prevention of back pain, and flexibility improvement (Mayo Clinic Staff, n.d.).

Stretching and flexibility exercises help, but the help of a massage therapist can loosen tight muscles, work out embedded knots or pockets of toxins, and help to improve and restore flexibility and mobility of joints and muscles. Massages on a regular basis for individuals from those with office jobs to health-care professionals have become a necessity instead of a luxury. Massages can augment daily stretching and flexibility exercises and work out deep embedded pockets of lactic acid, break up adhesions, and set the basis for

productive chiropractic adjustments. Stiff, unyielding tendons, ligaments, and muscles impede the successful treatment of chiropractic
care. At times I have had no improvement in chiropractic treatments
from stiff unyielding muscles, ligaments, and tendons in spite of
stretching and flexibility exercises until I had a massage before my
chiropractic adjustments.

Appendix 7

My Experience with Meridian Assessment Tools

Meridians are channels or conduits of energy detected along the pathway of the nerves. These meridians are the same channels called acupuncture points and accessed during acupressure. The Meridian Stress Assessment (MSA) uses BioMeridian testing or electrodermal screening, which measures the acupuncture meridian energy levels ("Meridian Stress Assessment—A Powerful Tool," 2010). This energy carries information about the condition of internal organs and systems. "Biomeridian's MSA is the only FDA approved Class II system that uses electro-acupuncture technology to accurately assess meridian dysfunction" (ibid.). Approximately every two months, I have an MSA test done. The BioMeridian testing has been used to indicate the state of weakness or strength of organs, emotional imprints experienced such as anger, sadness, frustration, or happiness, and the exposure to viruses, bacteria, mold, fungus, and so on. I had my pineal gland's energy level evaluated to determine if the measures to enhance my melatonin levels had been effective. The results indicated that the reading of my pineal gland was only off by one point. The health consultant who conducted the MSA indicated the reading was not indicative of a weakened pineal gland. *My measures to promote sleep and health and wellness have been beneficial and worth the effort.*

Notes

Notes

About the Author

am a wife of thirty-four years, a mother of three awesome individuals, and a grandmother of five beautiful grandchildren. I graduated from Louisiana State University with an associate degree in nursing in 1983. In the year 2012, I fulfilled a promise I made to myself by going back to college and earning my Bachelor of Science degree in Nursing. Coworkers would often tell me I should go into education, since I was knowledgeable about healthier options of foods. I felt that many illnesses and diseases can be avoided or lessened by healthier choices, lifestyles and nutritional modifications. I enrolled in and later graduated from the Institute for Integrative Nutrition® (IIN) as a Health Coach. As a health Coach, I help clients put the brake on unhealthy lifestyles, develop individualized plans for diet and lifestyle changes, identify roadblocks, and develop individualized strategies to achieve goals and intentions. While complementing health-care providers; we assist individuals to take responsibility for their health. Health Coaches do not treat or diagnose; we do strive to direct clients how to develop their own health and wellness plans. Each individual is unique and has bioindividual properties. What works for one person may not work for someone else.

How could a health coach be of service to you?
Your Action Plan—Putting Tools into Action

1.

2.

3.

4.

5.

6.

7.

8.

9.

10.

REFERENCES

American Heart Association. " Body Composition Tests." Updated march, 18, 2014, accessed February 23, 2015. http://www.heart.org/HEARTORG/GettingHealthy/NutritionCenter/Body-Composition-Tests_UCM_305884_Article.jsp.

American Heart Association. "Sugar 101." Accessed May 5, 2015, http://www.heart.org/HEARTORG/Gettinghealthy/NutritionCenter/HealthyEating/Sugar-101_UCM_306024_Article.jsp.

American Nutrition Association. 2006. "The Science of Probiotics." 37(2), 2-6. Quoted from NOHA Oak Park lecture by Carlos Reynes, (February 8, 2005). Accessed February 25, 2015, http://americannutritionassociation.org/newsletter/sciences-probiotics.

Aranceta, Bartina J. and C. Perez-Rodrigo, 2013. Abstract: Association between Sucrose Intake and ancer: A Review of the Evidence. *PubMed-National Center for Biotechnology Information*, *4*, 95–105. Accessed November 15, 2014, doi: 10.3305/nh.28.28.sup4.6802.

Burron, Alice. 2014. *Why Sleep-Deprived Night Shift Nurses Gain Weight*. Accessed February 25, 2015, http://www.nursetogether.com/shift-workers-sleep-deprivation-and-weight-gain

Carolina Center for Integrative Medicine. 2010. "Meridian Stress Assessment-A Powerful Tool." Accessed January 2, 2015, https://www.carolinecenter.com/meridian-stress-assessment---a-powerful-tool.html.

Danilyan, Liliya. 2012. "The Healing Power of Detox: 10 Toxic Foods & 10 Healing Foods." *MindBodyGreen*. Accessed February 26, 2015. http://www.mindbodygreen.com/0-4592/The-Healing-Power-of-Detox-10-Toxic-Foods-10-Healing-Foods.html.

Dagnelli.Christine. 2013. Serotonin-Rich Foods. *Livestrong*. Last updated August 16, 2013. Accessed February 25, 2015. http://www.livestrong.com/article/261416-serotonin-rich-foods/.

Harvard Health Publication. 2006. " Importance of Sleep: Six Reasons not to Scrimp on Sleep." Accessed November 27, 2014. http://www.health.harvard.edu/press_releases/importance_of_sleep_and_health.

Heal With Food. (n.d.). "Healing Properties of Watercress." Para. 1,2,3. Accessed February 26, 2015, http://www.healwithfood.org/articles/watercress-oldest-healing-food.php.

Healthline Editorial Team. 2013. "The Benefits of Vitamin D." Accessed December 05, 2014, http://healthline.com/health/food-nutrition/benefits-vitamin-d#Overview1.

Howatson, Glyn, et al. 2011. Effects of Tart Cherry Juice (Prunus Cerasus) on Melatonin Levels and Enhanced Sleep Quality. *European Journal of Nutrition*. (2012) 51-909-916. Accessed May 13, 2015. Doi 10.1007/s00394-011-0263-7.

Huffington Post. 2012. "Sleep Deprivation Could Spur Hormonal Changes Linked with Obesity, Review". Last updated October 26, 2012. Accessed March 05, 2015, http://huffingtonpost.com/2012/10/26/sleep-deprivation-obesity-leptin-ghrelin-insulin_n_2007043.html.

Inverarity, Laura. (n.d.). "Stretching 101: Benefits and Proper Techniques." Accessed May 5, 2015, http://physicaltherapy.about.com/od/flexibilityexercises/a/stretchbasics.htm

Kaczor, Tina. 2010. An Overview of Melatonin and Breast Cancer-Exploring Melatonin's Unique Effects on Breast Cancer Cells. *Natural Medicine Journal*. 2(2). Accessed November 25, 2014, http://naturalmedicinejournal.com/2010-02/overview-melatonin-and-breast-cancer.

Mayo Clinic Staff. 2014. *Healthy Lifestyle Fitness.* Accessed February 26, 2015. http://www.mayoclinic.org/healthy-living/fitness/in-depth/pilates-for-beginners/art-20047673?pg=1.

Mayo Clinic Staff. 2013. Stress Management. *Healthy Lifestyle.* Para .8. Accessed February 25, 2015. http://www.mayoclinic.org/healthy-living/stress-management/in-depth/stress/art-20046037.

McCune, L. M., C. Kubota, N. R. Stendell-Hollis, and C. A. Thomson. 2011. Cherries and Health: A Review. *Critical Review Food Science Nutrition. 51*(1), 1–12. Accessed December 12, 2014. doi:10.1080/10408390903001719.

McDermott, Nicole. 2014. The Benefits of Vitamin B complex. *Life by Daily Burn.* Accessed February 24, 2015, http://dailyburn.com/life/health/benefits-vitamin-b-complex/.

Mileva, G., Baker, S.L., Konkle, A. T., and Bielajew, C. 2014. "Abstract: Bisphenol-A: Epigenetic reprogramming and effects on reproduction and behavior." *International Journal of Environmental Research and Public Health, 11*(7), 7537–61. Accessed February 26, 2015. doi: 10.3390/ijerph110707537.

Nall, Rachel. 2013. The Normal Time for Food Digestion. *Livestrong.* Accessed February 24, 2015. http://www.livestrong.com/article/525519-the-normal-time-for-food-to-process-through-the-bowels-colon/.

National Cancer Institute. (n.d.). "Garlic and Cancer." Reviewed January 22, 2008. Accessed February 26, 2015, http://www.cancer.gov/cancertopics/causes-preentio/risk-factors/diet/garlic-fact-sheet.

National Cancer Institute. (n.d.). "Cruciferous Vegetables and Cancer Prevention." Reviewed June 7, 2012. Accessed February 26, 2015, http://www.cancer.gov/cancertopics/causes-prevention/risk-factors/diet/cruciferous-vegetables-fact-sheet.

National Sleep Foundation. 2014. "What Happens When You Sleep." Accessed February 23, 2015. http://sleepfoundation.org/how-sleep-works/what-happens-when-you-sleep.

Price, Michael. 2011. The risks of Night Work. *Monitor on Psychology*, 42(1), 38. Accessed November 25, 2014. http://www.apa.org/monitor/2011/01/night-work.aspx.

Renter, Elizabeth. 2013. 8 Foods to Naturally Increase Melatonin for Better Sleep. *Natural Society*. Accessed December 17, 2014. http://naturalsociety.com/8-foods-naturally-increase-melatonin-sleep/.

Roehrs, Timothy and Roth, Thomas. (n.d.). Sleep, Sleepinesss, and Alcohol Use. *NIH-National Institute on alcohol Abuse and Alcoholism*. Accessed December 21, 2014, https://www.pubs.niaaa.nih.gpv/publications/arh25-2/-101-109.htm.

Rosenthal, J. (2007). *Integrative Nutrition: Feed Your Hunger for Health & Happiness*. Austin, TX: Greenleaf Book Group, LLC.

Sargis, Robert. 2014. An Overview of the pineal Gland. Maintaining Circadian Rhythym. *Endocrineweb*. Accessed April 25, 2015. www.endocrine web.com/endocrinology/overview-pineal-gland.

Schor, Jacob. 2012. Cherry Juice Supplies Melatonin and Improves Sleep. *Natural Medicine Journal*. 4 (5) 2. Accessed May 13, 2015. http://naturalmedicinejournal.com/journal/2012-05/cherry-juice-supplies-melatonin-and-improves-sleep.

Sisson, Mark. 2012. *The PRIMAL BLUEPRINT. Reprogram Your Genes for Effortless Weight Loss, Vibrant Health, and Boundless Energy*. Malibu, CA: Primal Nutrition, Inc.

Smith, Mark R. and Eastman, Charmane I. 2012. Shift work: Health, Performance and Safety Problems, Traditional Countermeasures, and Innovative Management Strategies to Reduce Circadian Misalignment. *Nature and*

Science of Sleep, 4, 111–132. Accessed December 29, 2015. doi:10.2147/NSS. S10372.

Travis, Wendy. (n.d.). Bedtime Snacks That Help You Fall Asleep. *Lifescript-Healthy Living for Women.* Accessed on November 21, 2014, http://www. lifescript.com/diet-fitness/articles/archive/diet/eat-well/bedtime_snack_ that_help_you_fall_asleep.aspx

Tucker, Melanie D. 2014. Benefits of Deep Breathing. *Livestrong.* Accessed February 26, 2015. http://www.livestrong.com/article/ 92264-benefits-deep-breathing/

Turner, Natasha. 2013. "Six Hidden Health Benefits of Cherries." *Huffington Post.* Updated June 30, 2014. Accessed February 24, 2015, http://www. huffingtonpost.ca/natasha-turner-nd/cheeries-benefits_b_3757989. html.

U.S. National Library of Medicine National Institutes of Health. (n.d.). Enzyme. *MedlinePlus Medical Encyclopedia. Last updated January 21, 2013.* Accessed February 26, 2015, http://www.nlm.nih.gov/medlineplus/ency/ar-ticle/002353.htm

Van Cauter, Eve Van. Kristen Knutson, Rachel Leproult, and Karine Spiegel. 2005. The Impact of Sleep Deprivation on Hormones and Metabolism. *Medscape Nurses from Medscape Neurology-Insomnia and Sleep Health Expert Column.* 7, (1), para 9. Accessed December 14, 2014, http://www.medscape. org/viewarticles/502825_print.

Warner, Jennifer. (2005). Small Weight Loss Takes Big Pressure Off Knees. *WebMD Health News.* Sources: Messier, S. I. July, 2005; (52): 2026-2032. News Release, John Wiley & Sons Inc. Accessed February 26, 2015, http://www.webmd.com/osteoarthritis/news/ small-weight-loss-takes-pressure-off-knees.

Webmd. (n.d.). Melatonin-Overview. *Sleep Disorders Health Center.* Last modi-fied June 20, 2012. (Information taken from the National Cancer Institute by Webmd) Accessed December 16, 2014, http://www.webmd.com/sleep-disorders/tc/melatonin-overview.

Weil, Andrew. 2015. The 4-7-8 Breath: Health Benefits & Demonstration. *Dr. AndrewWeil.com*. Accessed February 26, 2015. http://www.drweil.com/drw/u/VDR00112/The-4-7-8-Breath-Benefits-and-Demonstration.html.

Woodyard, Catherine. 2011. Exploring the Therapeutic Effects of Yoga and its Ability to Increase Quality of Life. *International Journal of Yoga*, *4*(2), 49–54. Accessed February 26, 2015, doi: 10.4103/0973–6131.85485.

Zamosky, Lisa. (n.d.). *Food & Recipes The Truth About Tryptohan*. Accessed December 13, 2014, http://www.webmd.com/food-recipes/features/the-truth-about-tryptophan?print=true

www.ingramcontent.com/pod-product-compliance
Lightning Source LLC
Chambersburg PA
CBHW061457040426
42450CB00008B/1390